How do you draw **DINOSAURS?**

Especially for Raya —
happy dinosaur drawing!
Love,
DCDuBoyne
4·14·89

How do you draw
DINOSAURS?

by D. C. DuBosque

Peel Productions
Portland, Oregon

Library of Congress Cataloging-in-Publication Data

DuBosque, D. C. (Douglas C.)

    How do you draw dinosaurs? / by D. C. DuBosque
-- 1st ed.   p.   cm. -- (Growing books)
    Summary: An instruction book for drawing dinosaurs
of various types.
    ISBN 0-939217-10-4 (pbk.) : $6.95
    1. Dinosaurs in art--Juvenile literature. 2. Drawing--
Technique-Juvenile literature. [1. Dinosaurs in art.
2. Drawing-Technique.] I. Title II. Series
NC780.5.D84 1988
743'.6--dc19   88-25421

ISBN 0-939217-10-4

Contents

Foreword

Dinosaurs have always fascinated me. As a kid I was wild about them... I kept dinosaurs everywhere. Much later, during a more somber period of my life, living overseas and managing an international company, wearing business suits and driving a dark blue 4-door BMW, I still carried on the dashboard a bright orange, plastic Tyrannosaurus Rex. Now it lives atop my drawing board. It guards my pencils when I travel.

Now, as a children's book illustrator visiting schools, I hear from tens of thousands of kids how much they like dinosaurs, too. They all seem to ask, "How do you draw dinosaurs?"

This book answers their question. It's not just for them: it's also for their teachers, who may see in it outlines of lesson plans (no accident; I have taught students of all elementary and secondary levels); their school media specialists, who know that nothing pulls reluctant readers to the library like a good dinosaur; and their parents, many of whom have wondered aloud how to encourage their visually motivated offspring. (Take up drawing yourself!)

Adults don't ask "How do you draw?" but you can tell they want to. Several years ago, at a School of Visual Arts summer session in Morocco, I was astounded to find professional people (my fellow students) admiring my work and saying, "Gee, I wish I could draw." I just assumed, being graphic artists and designers, that they all drew, and probably a lot better than I could. I hope this book will find its way into some of their hands. I don't think the appeal of **How do you draw dinosaurs?** is limited to younger students by any means; I would love to have had a copy for reference when I studied at Brown University and Rhode Island School of Design!

Having mentioned that SVA summer session in Morocco, I should add that special thanks are due once again to the patient, inspiring, and eye-opening teachers there: Marshall Arisman, Eileen Hedy Schultz, Ed Benguiat, and Milton Glaser.

Introduction

Bones. That's all we have from dinosaurs. As you study dinosaurs, you'll learn that certain bones - the pubis, the ischium - are different in different dinosaurs - and perhaps you'll be told those bones make dinosaurs very different from animals like cows, dogs, and horses. Don't believe it.

Look at the skeleton of *Dienonychus*, or *Pentaceratops*, or *Stegosaurus*...and then look at a skeleton of a horse, a lion, a cow, an elephant. Put them side by side. What do you see? Ribs. Backbones. Rear leg bones start at the hip and point forward, then backwards, then forwards.

Front leg bones connect to a shoulder blade, then point backward, then forward. Skulls have eye sockets somewhere above a jaw that hinges open - just like your own. All creatures with internal skeletons - including birds and fish - have extraordinary similarities.

As you draw dinosaurs, then, you'll discover much about how all animals, and people, are put together. As you draw dinosaurs, look at the evidence (bones), look at other illustrators' ideas, borrow the techniques I'll show you, and then look, and draw, and draw some more!

Preparation

Have plenty of clean, white paper handy. I collect used computer and photocopy paper for my practice drawings. I buy #1 pencils at an office supply store. They work well, and cost less than artists' pencils. Use spray fixative (hair spray might also work) to prevent smudging on drawings you want to keep. Keep a pencil sharpener right next to you, and use it often. Use an eraser just to "clean up," not to "fix." Keep drawing over mistakes until the page is a complete mess and then reach for a new sheet.

Relax your body

Before you draw, take a few minutes to breathe deeply, move and stretch. Do a few shoulder rolls (forward and back, slowly,) then some head tilts (forward and back and to both sides.) Then stand up and take a deep breath, stretching your arms high, bringing them down while breathing out. Put your fists together, and slowly twist your torso to both sides. Touch your toes. Look at colors and shadows upside down!

Relax your eyes

Rub the palms of your hands together ten or twenty times and gently place them over your eyes, blacking out any light but not touching your eyelids. Relax; breathe deeply and quietly until all you can see is smooth, even black. It might take a while, so rest your elbows on a table or desk if you need to. When you're ready, take your hands away and marvel at how vivid colors and shapes look. Do it before and after drawing.

Part I: Building an easy animal, step by step

Here's an animal you can see alive, in action at the zoo (at feeding time if you're lucky), at the circus, or on TV. You won't have that chance with a dinosaur (unless you know something I don't.) Watching an elephant, you can imagine what large dinosaurs looked like in motion. Practice drawing elephants, and try to watch a real elephant - it will help your dinosaur drawing!

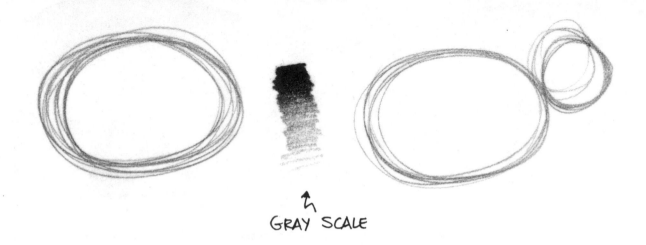

GRAY SCALE

Start with ovals - very lightly, over and over. Do plenty of them. Try holding the pencil different ways - straight up and down on the paper, sideways like chalk for writing on a chalkboard... when you get an oval you like, add another oval for the head.

Do your ovals have flat spots in them, like mine? That's OK - most animals have flat spots too. Practice drawing "gray scales" - how dark, and how light, can you mark with the pencil and paper you're using? *Always start by drawing lightly!*

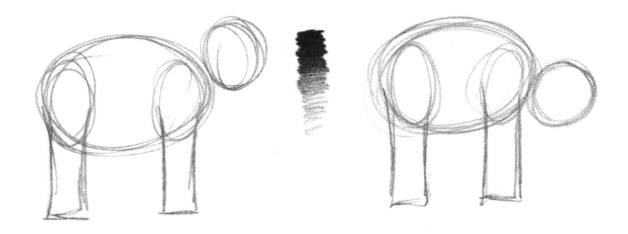

Before you add legs, draw two ovals where the legs will "attach" to the body. *If your drawing doesn't look good to you, remember this: people who say "I can't draw" are like people who say "I can't swim." What they mean is they've never learned, and they're probably afraid to try. Loosen up! Have fun!*

Try drawing the ovals again - on the same sheet, on the back of the paper, even on another sheet - and this time, put the head a little lower. That's all - keep it simple.

After all, we're just practicing. These drawings aren't supposed to be perfect! Now try again, this time with the head held higher. If you're using fresh sheets of paper each time, save the old ones for drawing practice ovals, drawing gray scales, or doodling.

Can you make your animal stand on its rear legs?

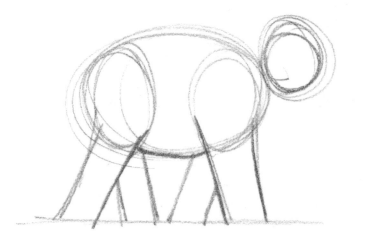

Still drawing *very lightly*, try a more challenging pose. Note the position of the legs in these two drawings. Practice these drawings until you have them memorized, and you'll have little trouble making your dinosaurs "walk."

Don't go on until you've drawn each of these several times - draw quickly or slowly, but make sure you're comfortable with your ability to draw a walking animal.

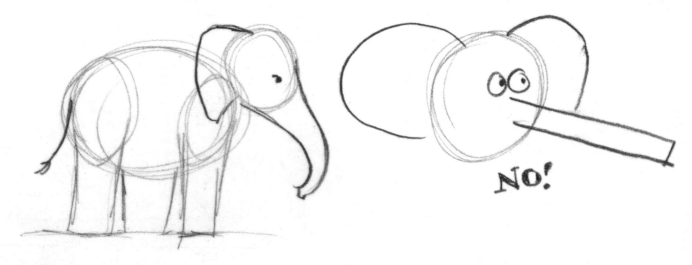

NO!

Add the tail, the ear and eye (one each when you're looking from the side), and the trunk. *No Pinocchio noses!*

Here are some other ideas for elephants: make one with its head low and the trunk stretching down (as if drinking water.) Make another with its head held up, and trunk stretching up (as if eating out of a tree.) Make an elephant spraying water on its back! Put the legs in different positions as you draw the different elephants.

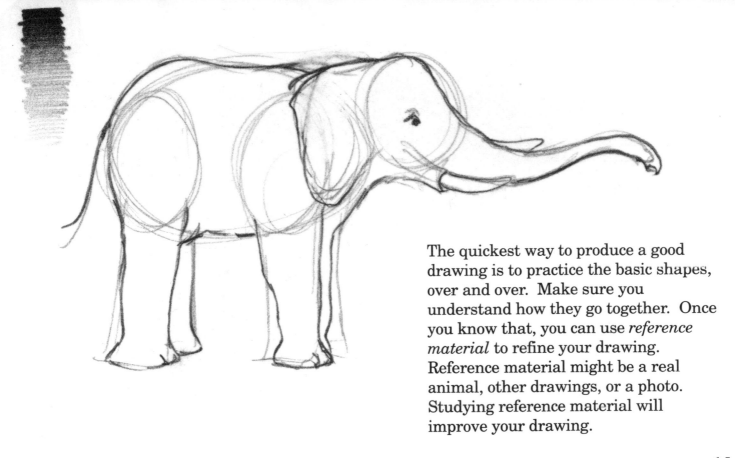

The quickest way to produce a good drawing is to practice the basic shapes, over and over. Make sure you understand how they go together. Once you know that, you can use *reference material* to refine your drawing. Reference material might be a real animal, other drawings, or a photo. Studying reference material will improve your drawing.

TEST!

Put your drawings away.

Take a clean sheet of paper, a sharp pencil, and draw from memory:

- a standing elephant, and

- a walking elephant.

Close this book before you start. Open it again when you're through.

Was it difficult? If so, close your eyes and remember, step by step, the shapes you used to draw the elephant. Now try again.

Was it easy? Congratulations! You're using your mind to think in pictures - this is an important part of drawing.

Next look at light and shadow. There are two types of shadows. Light causes us to see both.

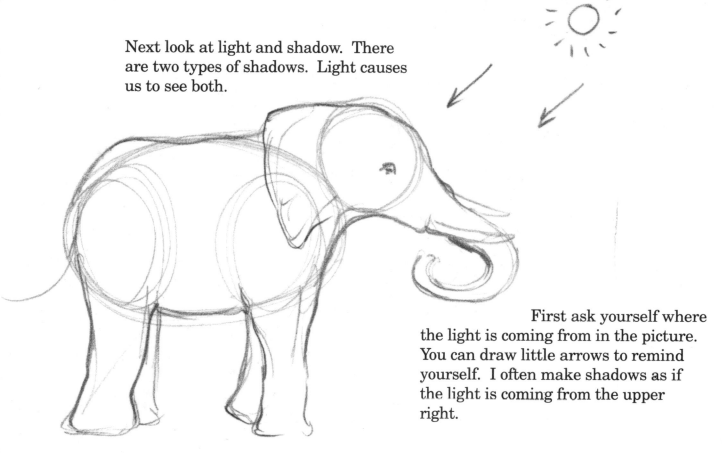

First ask yourself where the light is coming from in the picture. You can draw little arrows to remind yourself. I often make shadows as if the light is coming from the upper right.

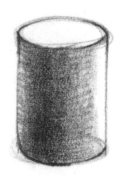

To get good at shading, try the sphere and the cylinder. Important practice shapes, they'll make shading an elephant (or a dinosaur) much easier. With different drawings of the sphere and cylinder, have the light coming from different directions. A real egg is a great subject for studying shadows!

The first shadow to draw is on the object (in this case, on the elephant.) It's called the contour shadow, because it follows the contours (the shape) of the object. Use different shades of gray in this shadow; here's where your own gray scale (you did draw one, didn't you?) is a handy reference.

The second shadow is a cast shadow (*cast* means *thrown;* the shadow is *thrown* on the ground). The cast shadow doesn't need to be perfect - it just has to look good! Make sure it touches the object, or the object will appear to be floating (or jumping, or flying, or dropping)!

You can see how the two types of shadows work together. Near the ground, they run right into each other.

You can see, too, how the gray scale in the upper left hand corner reminds you how dark and how light you can draw with the pencil and paper you're using.

LIGHT

There are many varieties of shadows you can draw. Look for new ideas. How about a l-o-o-n-n-g cast shadow, like you'd see in early morning or late after-noon. Which does this look like - early morning or late afternoon? Why? What would the shadow of a tree look like in this type of lighting?

Un-
SCIENTIFIC AMERICAN

ELEPHANTOSAURUS

ARTIST'S CONCEPTION OF THIS RECENTLY ~~INVENTE~~ DISCOVERED DINOSAUR

Part II: Drawing "easy" dinosaurs

This is your time to draw, so I won't distract you with too many instructions. Just questions, OK?

If you have trouble with any of the drawings that follow, you may want to :
- *practice the basic shapes,*
- *look more closely at the example, and*
- *try again!*

Did any *Stegosaurus* have six points on its tail? Where can you find out?

Would a *Stegosaurus* have eaten flowers? Are you sure?

Notice how the big oval you drew be-
comes more like a pear shape - the [front?]
legs are shorter than the rear l[egs?]

...s reminds me of a rhinoceros named ...t Wildlife Safari Park in Oregon. ...ears like curved funnels.

Are scientists sure *Triceratops* didn't have ears? How would they know?

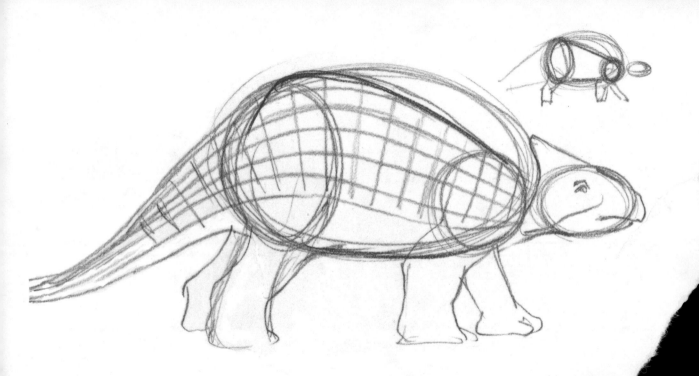

You'll certainly want to practice d
ing anklyo-bumps before puttin
on your dinosaur. Use a corr
paper, or a separate sheet

Most *Anklyosaurus* drawings show big spiky projections on the sides of their bodies. I based this drawing on an illustration that didn't show spikes.

Why might one illustrator draw bumps, where other illustrators draw spikes?

29

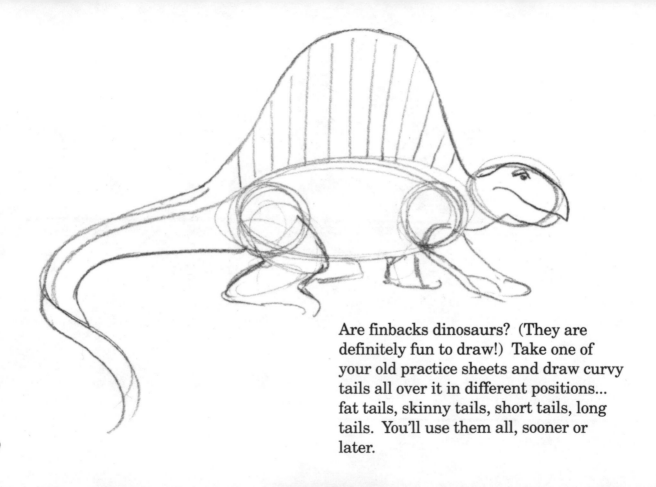

Are finbacks dinosaurs? (They are definitely fun to draw!) Take one of your old practice sheets and draw curvy tails all over it in different positions... fat tails, skinny tails, short tails, long tails. You'll use them all, sooner or later.

Do you always need to erase your practice lines? Here, they seem to make *Dimetrodon* look more alive, as if it's moving....

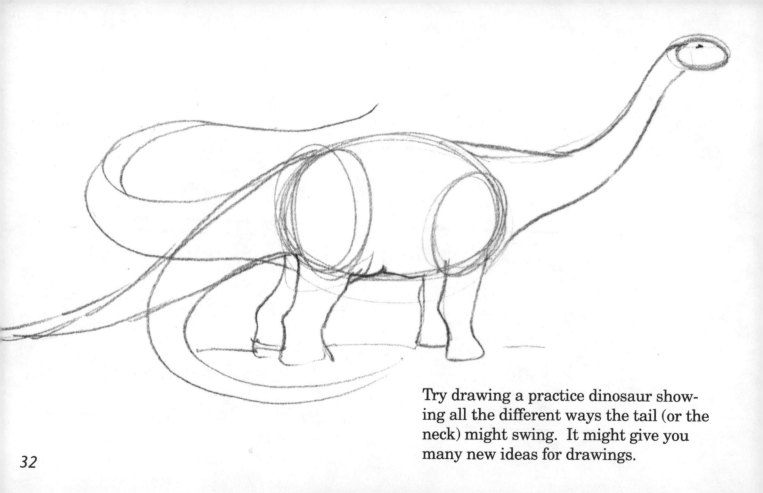

Try drawing a practice dinosaur show-
ing all the different ways the tail (or the
neck) might swing. It might give you
many new ideas for drawings.

Is this an *Apatosaurus? Brontosaurus?*
Brachiosaurus? Diplodocus?
Emseeyescherosaurus?

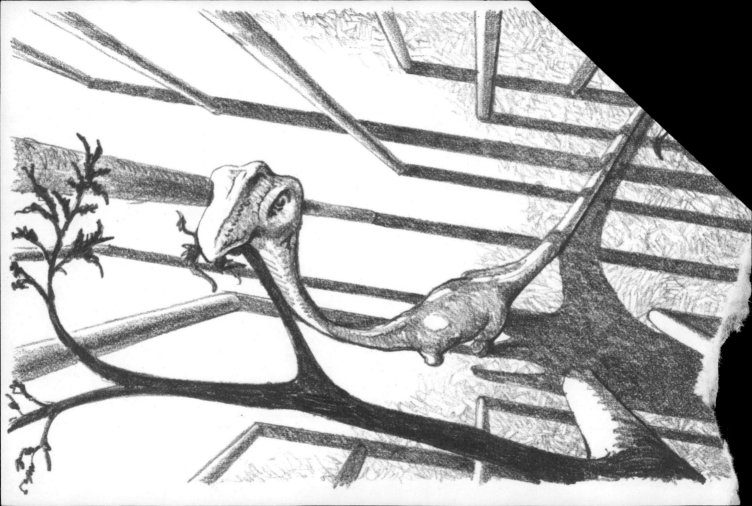

Part III: Drawing more complicated dinosaurs

Here I'll repeat my earlier advice - if you find any of these drawings difficult, you may want to:

- *spend more time practicing the basic shapes and how they're put together,*
- *look more closely at my examples, or at other reference material, and*
- *keep trying!*

left: *the trees are drawn using one-point perspective. The dinosaur is called Emseeyescherosaurus. You may not find any other reference material for this one; it's a rather rare dinosaur.*

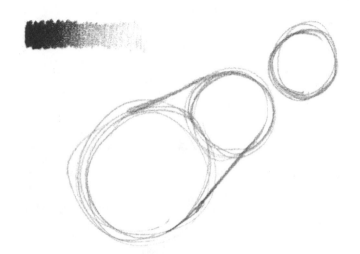

With more complex dinosaurs, it's often easiest to start with two ovals of different sizes, and connect them to make a pear shape.

Add another oval for the head. Remember, *draw lightly!* If you make a mistake, draw over it first. Mistakes are what learning is all about. If you start over, save the first sheet for practicing tails, or feet, or claws.

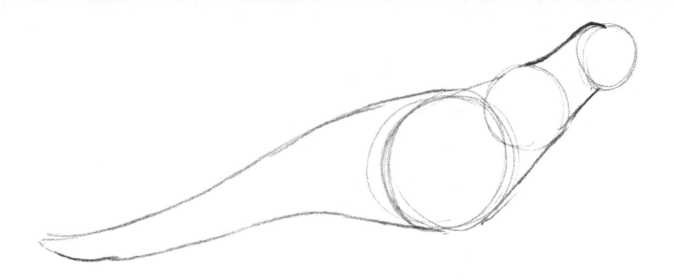

I've added two "S" curves for the tail. These are fun to draw. I make S-curve doodles all the time, on note pads, and when talking on the telephone. They're helpful when you want to draw plants, too. *Practice!*

Memorize this drawing.
(How? By drawing it, over and over
and over again until you've learned it!)

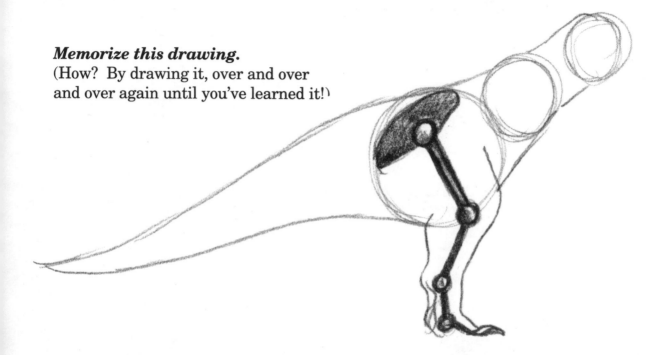

It shows you how the rear leg works -
on almost every walking or flying
animal you'll want to draw (except
insects.) The basic bending of the leg
is the same, though different animals'
feet vary a great deal.

If you want the memorizing to be more fun, make a "Leonardo Da Vinci" drawing like this: it shows over 60 different possible combinations of tail, legs, and upper body. That gives you all sorts of different drawings you can do - once you understand the basics!

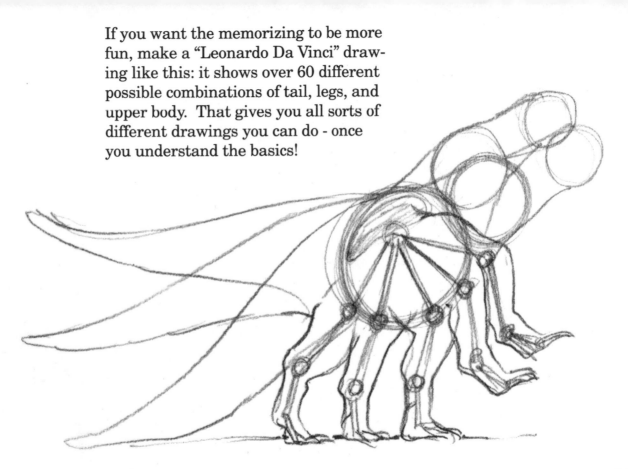

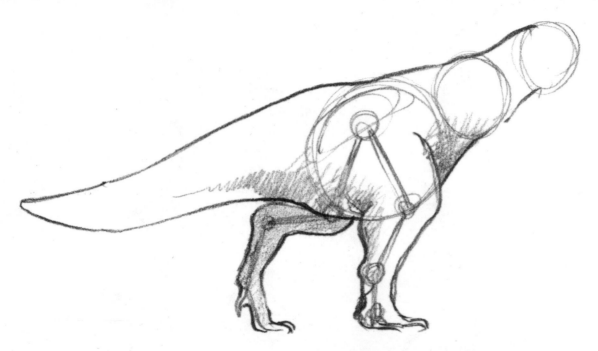

It takes practice and experience to know how and where to put shading - and you may choose not to put shading in every drawing. You certainly don't have to.

Like legs, arms bend almost the same way in a great number of animals. But they can be complicated, so it's helpful to have good reference material.

After all, on some animals you draw, the "arms" will be front legs, or wings, or even flippers!

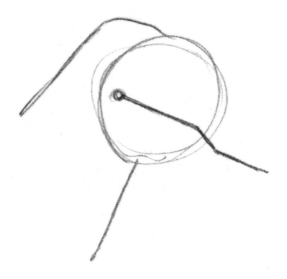

To draw the head of a carnivore like *Tyrannosaurus Rex* or *Allosaurus*, first notice how the neck connects to the circle or oval you've drawn for the head.

Next, notice where the mouth (jaw) hinges. This doesn't mean you'll see the mouth opening all the way back. Try this on your own jaw: feel in front of your ears where the jaw hinges, and then look in the mirror to see how far the opening of your mouth goes back towards it - not very far!

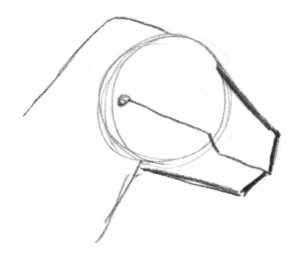

Keep the shapes as simple as you can, so that they'll be easy to remember. As you practice these shapes, you'll be surprised how easy it is to draw the head!

Add an eye, and a little peak for an eyebrow. Do scientists know for sure that this dinosaur would have a peaked eyebrow?

Practice!   See if you can draw a head with the mouth open. Don't worry about shading and details; just concentrate on getting the "mechanics" of it right.

Sometimes turning your paper helps. After drawing the upper jaw, you could rotate the paper slightly to draw the lower jaw. Nothing says the paper always has to be straight up and down!

After doing this drawing, I knew something was wrong - I didn't know what. Some people would just crumple the paper or throw it out if they knew something was wrong with their drawing. I didn't. I kept it, though I didn't enjoy looking at it. I wanted to find out why it looked so bad to me. Finally, in a dinosaur book, I saw the problem: I hadn't given the dinosaur enough of a throat. I wanted to fix that idea in my mind, but I didn't want to do the drawing all over, so I drew right on top of the old drawing. It doesn't look great, but I'll hang onto it: it's great reference material for the next time I want to draw a carnivorous dinosaur with its mouth wide open.

There are all sorts of dinosaurs similar
to Tyrannosaurus Rex and Allosaurus,
some of them quite small. They could
be tiny Compsognatus, or an ostrich-
like coelurosaur such as
Dromiceiomimus...

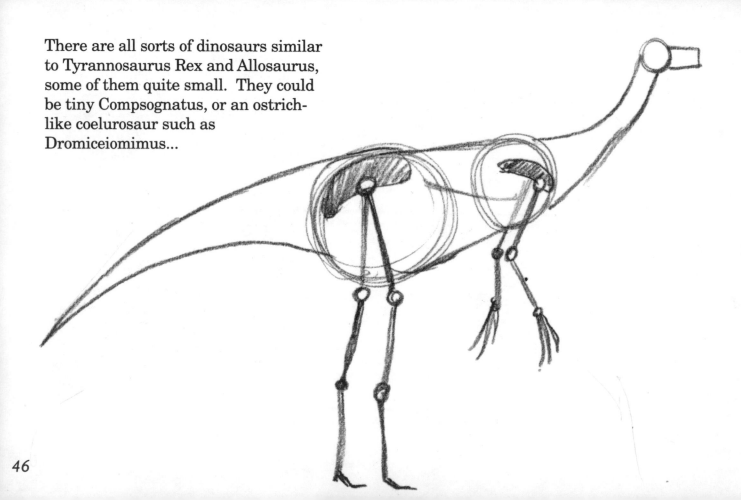

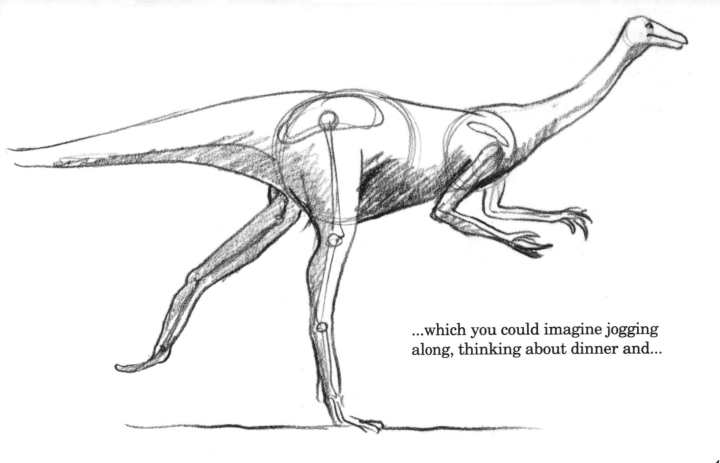

...which you could imagine jogging along, thinking about dinner and...

...spotting a tasty morsel on the wing, and...

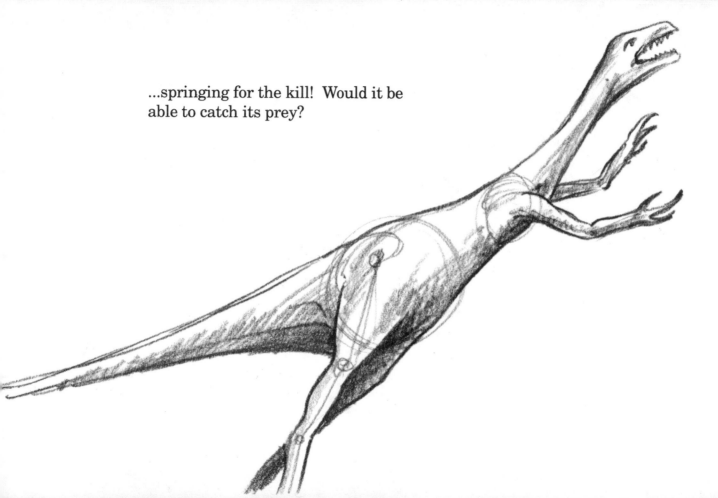

...springing for the kill! Would it be
able to catch its prey?

You bet!

Part IV: Adding new angles to your drawings

With what you've learned so far about constructing body shapes, articulating tails, legs, and arms, and building heads, you should be able to draw some impressive dinosaurs! The next step is to observe and practice drawing the same animals from different angles. You need to use more visual imagination, but you're only limited by how much time you're willing to devote to studying and practicing!

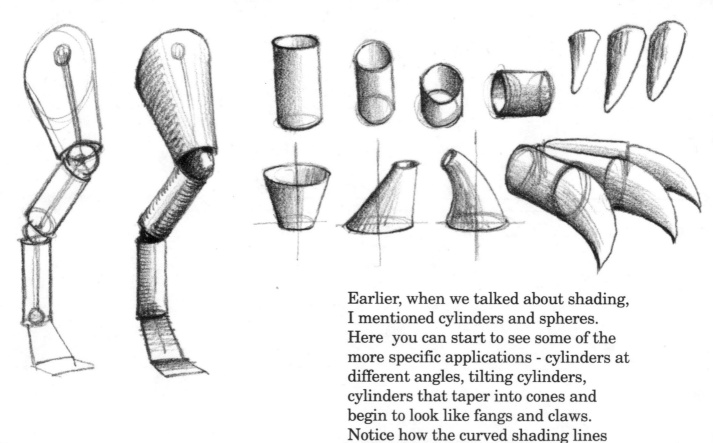

Earlier, when we talked about shading, I mentioned cylinders and spheres. Here you can start to see some of the more specific applications - cylinders at different angles, tilting cylinders, cylinders that taper into cones and begin to look like fangs and claws. Notice how the curved shading lines help make them "round."

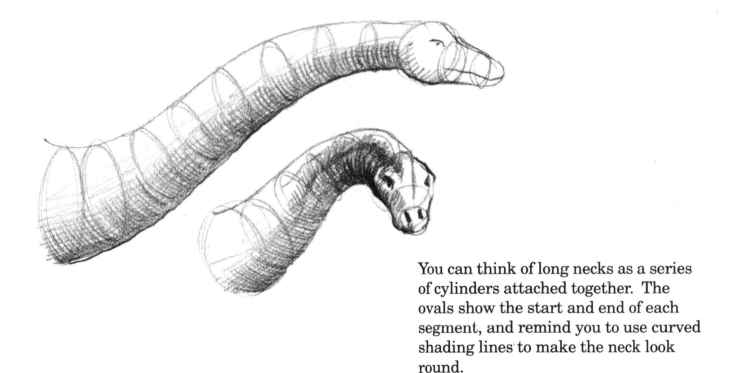

You can think of long necks as a series of cylinders attached together. The ovals show the start and end of each segment, and remind you to use curved shading lines to make the neck look round.

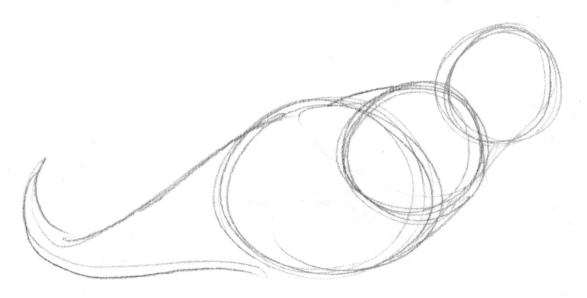

To draw a dinosaur facing towards
you, start with the same ovals you
drew earlier - only this time, imagine
them three dimensional, like balloons
or soap bubbles. Let the ovals overlap
on the page.

This drawing shows how I visualize the
moving parts of the dinosaur.

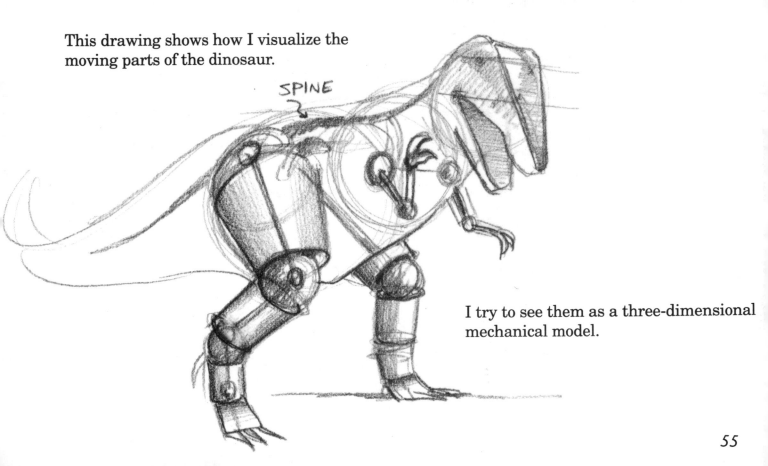

SPINE

I try to see them as a three-dimensional
mechanical model.

This is a practice drawing is a mess -
fast and sloppy. But with complicated
subjects, this type of drawing helps me
sort out the details, to see what's
important and what's not. It's fun, and
valuable as a learning tool!

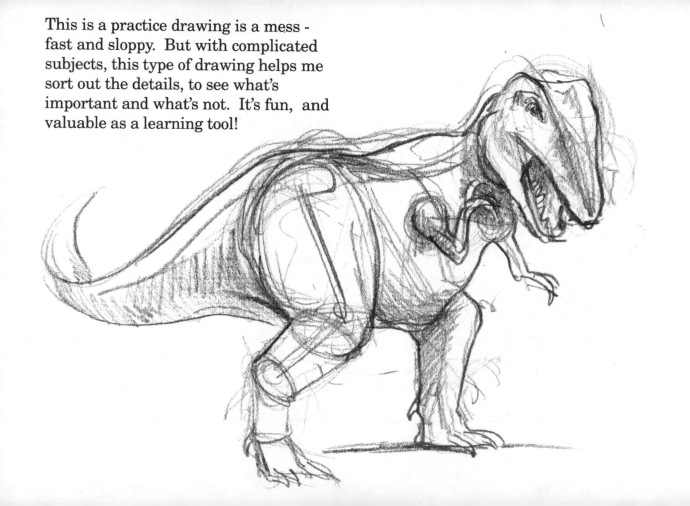

To finish this drawing, I'd carefully erase the few practice lines, then keep adding shadow and texture. This alone wouldn't make a great picture - you'd probably want to add some plants, and perhaps other animals.

In this sequence, I try to make *Triceratops* look easy to draw. It isn't. It took forever to get the horns and mouth in the right place and position, and I'm still not sure they're right. You may find in your drawings that certain details seem to hold you back.

Just keep trying! It's helpful to keep tracing paper on hand; you can draw different ideas on the tracing paper, lay them over the drawing and experiment before adding to the actual drawing. If you mess up, you can quickly transfer the "good" parts of a drawing to a new sheet to start again.

If you're not happy with your drawing, realize that other people might love your "terrible" drawings! And, if you're like me, you'll probably love your "terrible" drawings too, sooner or later.

Put them in your portfolio, and look at them after a week. You'll be amazed how much they've improved with age!

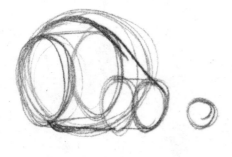

Stegosaurus is another dinosaur that's tricky to draw at an angle - those plates on the back can be very frustrating.

Don't expect your drawings to be perfect, because they may never be. Do expect your drawings to be good, simply because that happens naturally as you become better at observing and drawing basic shapes.

Always look for things you think you can't draw, and ask yourself why not - most likely, you simply need to look closer, or for a little longer. If you've been drawing slowly on a small sheet of paper, try one or two fast drawings on big pieces of paper. Relax your eyes and stretch.

*Constantly look at things and practice drawing them. When you have a few minutes with nothing to do - say, waiting for a bus - look at what's around you and simply **imagine** you're drawing it - that will make you good, <u>fast!</u>*

Here's a simple and inexpensive
portfolio you can make to store your
drawings. Make additional portfolios
as you need them. Save some "terrible"
drawings so you can watch yourself
improve!

USE STRING OR
SHOELACES TO TIE
PORTFOLIO CLOSED

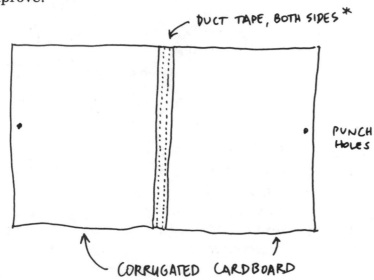

← DUCT TAPE, BOTH SIDES *

PUNCH
HOLES

CORRUGATED CARDBOARD

* LEAVE ABOUT ½" BETWEEN
CARDBOARD PIECES WHEN
TAPING SO THERE WILL BE
SPACE INSIDE FOR DRAWINGS!

Oh, yes...there is one other thing. You might have noticed that all the dinosaurs in this book face to the right. That is no accident. You see, I figured you might just draw everything in this book, follow all my suggestions, and still run out of things to draw. So here's a project for you: draw all the dinosaurs (and the elephants) facing the *other* way. It may be simple, and then again....

ORDER FORM

If you can't find **How do you draw dinosaurs?** in your bookstore, you can order direct from the publisher.

Name _____

Address _____

City _____ State _____ ZIP _____

_____ **How do you draw dinosaurs?**
$8.45 (US $6.95 + $1.50 postage and handling)

_____ Additional copies
$7.45 each ($6.95 + 50¢ postage and handling)

Mail order form and payment (check or money order) to:
Peel Productions, PO Box 11500-D, Portland, OR 97211-1500
Allow 3-4 weeks for delivery.